But Is It Art?

Body Art

Alix Wood

 Gareth Stevens
PUBLISHING

Please visit our website, **www.garethstevens.com**. For a free color catalog of all our high-quality books, call toll free 1-800-542-2595 or fax 1-877-542-2596.

Library of Congress Cataloging-in-Publication Data

Wood, Alix.
Body art / by Alix Wood.
p. cm. — (But is it art?)
Includes index.
ISBN 978-1-4824-2279-5 (pbk.)
ISBN 978-1-4824-2280-1 (6-pack)
ISBN 978-1-4824-2277-1 (library binding)
1. Body marking — Juvenile literature. 2. Body painting — Juvenile literature.
3. Body art — Juvenile literature. I. Wood, Alix. II. Title.
N6494.B63 W66 2015
391.6—d23

2527

First Edition

Published in 2015 by
Gareth Stevens Publishing
111 East 14th Street, Suite 349
New York, NY 10003

© Alix Wood Books
Produced for Gareth Stevens by Alix Wood Books
Designed by Alix Wood
Editor: Eloise Macgregor

Photo credits:
Cover, 1, 5, 8, 9, 11 right, 14, 16 left, 17, 19, 21 bottom, 22, 23, 25 bottom, 28, 29, 32 © Shutterstock; 4 © Luisa Puccini/Shutterstock; 6 © holbox/Shutterstock; 7 © Malgorzata Kistryn/Shutterstock; 10 © Greg James of Tattoos Deluxe; 11 left © Pavel L Photo and Video; 12 © Samsara; 13 © nevenm/Shutterstock; 15 top © Everett Collection/Shutterstock; 15 bottom © Jessie Tarbox Beals; 16 top © Amy Nichole Harris/Shutterstock; 17 © Einat Dan/www.bodypainting-festival.com; 18 top © Gryffindor; 18 bottom © Art Institute of Chicago; 20 © Alamy; 21 top © Thomas Willemsen; 24 top © Courtesy Julien's Auctions/M2MPR; 24 bottom © Sergey Lavrentev; 25 top © sherwood/Shutterstock; 26 top © Angelo Giampiccolo; 26 bottom left © Rulon Oboev; 26 bottom right © Michele Alfieri/Shutterstock; 27 © Nicor

Printed in the United States of America
CPSIA compliance information: Batch # CW15GS: For further information contact Gareth Stevens, New York, New York at 1-800-542-2595.

Contents

What Is Body Art?................................ 4

Conforming or Not? 6

Henna Tattoos.................................... 8

Tattoos...10

Body Piercings 12

Art on Nails and Teeth! 14

Body Painting....................................16

Masks 18

Art Using Your Body! 20

Can Makeup Be Art? 22

Special Effects 24

Body Modification 26

Is Body Art Art?................................28

Glossary..30

For More Information 31

Index 32

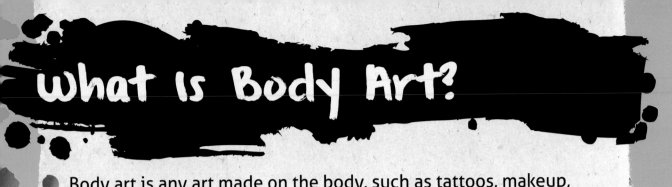

Body art is any art made on the body, such as tattoos, makeup, or body paint. It can be art that is made with the body as a kind of performance art. Or it can be art made to decorate the body, such as a mask.

People have been decorating their bodies for thousands of years. Body art was used as a way of identifying people belonging to your tribe, or to show their **status**. Some people believed it could provide magical protection against evil. It was thought to make people more attractive, too.

Arty Fact

Experts who study human societies believe that every **culture** on the planet has created some kind of body art at some time!

The Karo tribe from Ethiopia draw on their bodies with white chalk.

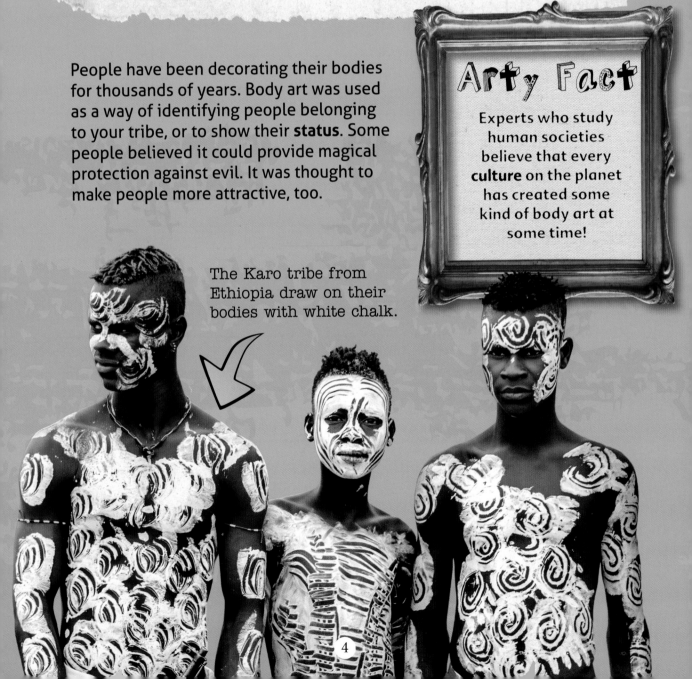

4

In modern times body art is mainly used as

- a form of self-expression
- an expression of spiritual belief
- a fashion statement
- a way to improve looks
- a **rite of passage**
- a way of showing a person belongs to a group

Body art is one of the earliest forms of art. In Africa, 160,000-year-old pencils used to create body art have been discovered!

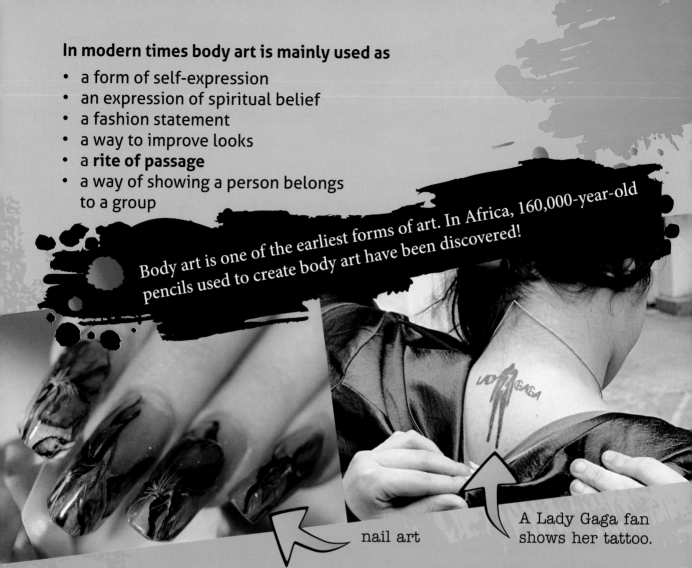

nail art

A Lady Gaga fan shows her tattoo.

WHAT DO YOU THINK?

Do you think the reason why someone has created body art affects whether it is really art or not? Is a beautiful nail design art? Is a band's name tattooed on a music fan art? Are they both art?

There are many definitions of what people think art is. Which of these do you agree with?

Art is:

- anything that an artist calls art

- something that is created with imagination and skill. It must be either beautiful, or express important ideas or feelings

- a mixture of "form" (the way something is created) and "content" (the "what" that has been created)

Conforming or Not?

To conform means to be the same as everyone else. A **nonconformist** stands out from the crowd. Body art can help a person feel **unique**. To be seen as art, the work should be original.

Some people like to feel part of the tribe. Some people prefer to feel unique. Warriors often wear elaborate masks to make them look more terrifying than their enemy. This mask makes the wearer look much taller than he actually is. It also helps disguise any fear on the warrior's own face. Is this traditional Mayan costume a work of art?

Arty Fact

Tattoos, makeup, or bodypaint become a mask to hide behind. Extreme body art can look threatening. Some people with body art like the reaction their extreme looks get from other people. The "mask" means that people are wary of them and leave them alone.

People often create body art to make them look different. We all make choices about what clothes we wear, or how we style our hair. Decorating our body is another way to display our own artistic style. Not all body art is unique self-expression, however. Sometimes people have body art done because it makes them feel part of a group. The fact that the art is the same as someone else's is important to them.

WHAT DO YOU THINK?

A little like when everyone in a group of friends wears a particular brand of sneakers, some people have tattoos to fit in. But you can change your sneakers. It's a lot harder to change a tattoo!

In some friend groups having a tattoo is not unique at all. Some rock bands or sports teams all have tattoos! Each individual tattoo could be art, though. Do you think these look like art?

There is a saying "good tattoos aren't cheap and cheap tattoos aren't good!" Great body artwork can be expensive.

Henna Tattoos

Henna tattoos are a fun and safe type of body art. They are not permanent. Henna is a paste made from leaves. The paste is used to draw patterns on skin. The dried paste is brushed away to leave the design behind. The longer the paste is left on, the stronger the color will be.

Henna tattoos are a tradition in India at weddings and religious ceremonies. Most henna artists work freehand and think up the designs as they go. The wearer and the artist are thought to develop a **spiritual** connection while the tattoo is being done.

Arty Fact

Many henna designs have particular meanings. Birds are messengers between heaven and earth. Flowers symbolize happiness. Eyes are meant to reflect evil, by turning any evil away from the wearer.

A Hindu bride has her palms tattooed with henna. Popular henna designs for the palms include sun and flower images.

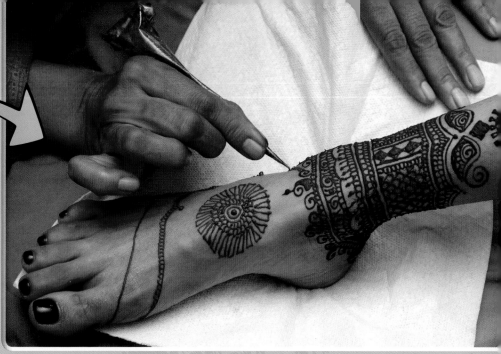

The feet are a spiritual place to have henna tattoos. The feet are believed to connect the body, mind, and spirit with the earth.

Talented henna artists charge high fees for their work. Countries such as India, Pakistan, Sri Lanka, Morocco, Yemen, Somalia, and Sudan have thriving henna businesses. Henna artists are very important in the **Hindu** community. On the night before a Hindu wedding the bride is decorated with henna. Sometimes, the name or initials of the groom are hidden within the design.

Henna designs are used in art, too.

WHAT DO YOU THINK?

Henna tattoos are a type of folk art. Folk art is decorative art created by ordinary people. Often the artists are self-taught. Some art collectors feel that folk art is not as worthy as fine art. Do you agree?

Tattoos

A tattoo is a type of body art. Tattoos are created by putting permanent ink into the skin to change the skin's color. Just like with painting styles, there are many different types of tattoos. Some people create really lifelike drawings; others create designs or **typography**.

Greg James is a well-known tattoo artist. His tattoo designs and artwork have been featured in magazines, books, and documentaries. As with many tattoo artists, he also creates other types of art. He designed a bass guitar for band Mötley Crüe, which now hangs in the Hard Rock Café in Tampa, Florida.

A tattoo by Greg James

Greg James on creating tattoos:
"It's permanent. You can't tear it up and throw it away when you're done with it."

Arty Fact

To become a tattoo artist, people usually work as an **apprentice** to an established artist. Apprentices learn about cleanliness and safety before they are allowed to work on a client.

Tattoos have become more popular in recent years and all types and ages of people are having them done. There are tattoo conventions where artists get together and showcase their skills. Art galleries have started holding exhibitions showing photographs of some of the best tattoo artists' work.

A tattooed sleeve design photographed at the Moscow International Tattoo Convention.

WHAT DO YOU THINK?

Tattoo artists either create freehand original tattoos or they copy images and trace them onto the customer's skin. Which do you think is most artistic, a brilliant copy, or a not so good original piece?

Some tattoos depict words instead of images. Are they as artistic?

Body Piercings

Body piercings have been practiced for thousands of years. Even ancient Egyptian mummies had their ears pierced! People have piercings for different reasons. Perhaps they think the piercing and its jewelry make them look better? Some pierce as part of their religion or culture. Other piercings are done as a statement. Which of these reasons would make them most likely to be art, do you think?

Sometimes piercings are used to show a person's status. The Khond women have their ears pierced all around the edges. Pieces of straw are stuck through the holes until the woman marries, when small brass rings replace the straw. These piercings are not really supposed to be art.

This Khond woman's piercings show she is married.

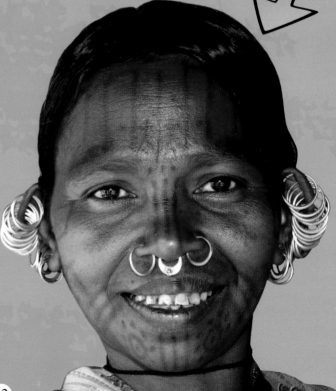

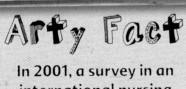

Arty Fact

In 2001, a survey in an international nursing publication asked people why they had had a piercing. They found that 62% of people had done it "to express their individuality."

Elaine Davidson has held the record for being the world's most pierced woman!

Elaine Davidson has around 9,000 piercings! She estimates that the rings and studs she wears weigh around 6.6 pounds (3 kg)! Like it or not, she has certainly created a unique look!

Piercing is a creative process. The client and the piercer have to decide where the piercing should go and what adornment to choose. It is a way of making a body stand out from the crowd. But some people do not like piercings. Several companies limit the amount of piercings employees can have. Some companies do not allow their employees to display piercings at all!

WHAT DO YOU THINK?

If people dislike the appearance of piercings, then does that mean that they are not art? Does art have to appeal to people? Or is it OK if art shocks or disgusts people?

Art on Nails and Teeth!

Nail art is a very popular type of body art. Most beauty salons will do some kind of nail art. People like to decorate themselves. Some people even decorate their teeth!

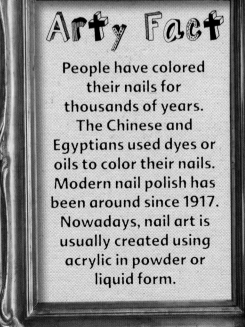

Nail artists get together at nail art conventions to compete and exhibit their work, such as at Tokyo's Nail Expo. Nail artists can create some stunning, original work. The art can be a little like creating a miniature painting. Most nail artists love art and consider that their work is creative.

Hand-painted original nail art

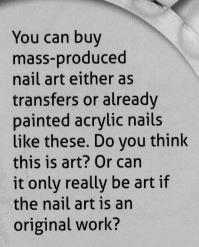

You can buy mass-produced nail art either as transfers or already painted acrylic nails like these. Do you think this is art? Or can it only really be art if the nail art is an original work?

Arty Fact

People have colored their nails for thousands of years. The Chinese and Egyptians used dyes or oils to color their nails. Modern nail polish has been around since 1917. Nowadays, nail art is usually created using acrylic in powder or liquid form.

14

There are a few arty ways to change the appearance of your teeth. A grill is a type of jewelry worn over the teeth. They are popular with hip hop artists and rappers. Grills are made of metal and sometimes inlaid with precious stones. They are usually removable. People can also get tooth tattoos! The tattoos are placed on a crown which is then fitted onto the teeth by a dentist.

Rap artist Chingy wearing a grill.

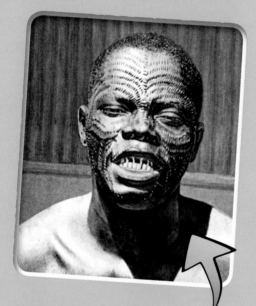

Some cultures sharpen their teeth to points! It is either done to make them more attractive or to resemble an animal, such as a shark.

WHAT DO YOU THINK?

Body art is often done as part of a culture's traditions, and not done purely for appearance. Both reasons, for culture or for appearance, can help the person feel they "fit in" to their group. Is that really art then, or something else?

Gold teeth are a way of showing someone's wealth with just a smile! They can be a symbol of status and power. If the person ran out of money they could always sell their teeth, too!

Body Painting

Body painting turns the human body into an artwork! It is one of the oldest forms of art. Body painting is believed to have been done in most tribal communities for thousands of years. It was often done for rituals and ceremonies.

Traditional tribal face paint from Papua New Guinea

Hunters paint their faces and bodies in **camouflage** paint, so that they can creep up on their prey unnoticed. Some body paint artists specialize in painting bodies that hide in their background, too. The paintings are very skillful. But body camouflage creates something that people can't see! Is that art? Perhaps the surprise when people realize someone is hiding is when it becomes art?

camouflage body paint

WHAT DO YOU THINK?

Is a hunter's camouflage paint art? When does camouflage painting stop being practical and start becoming art? This woman is not camouflaged for a practical reason. Is she art?

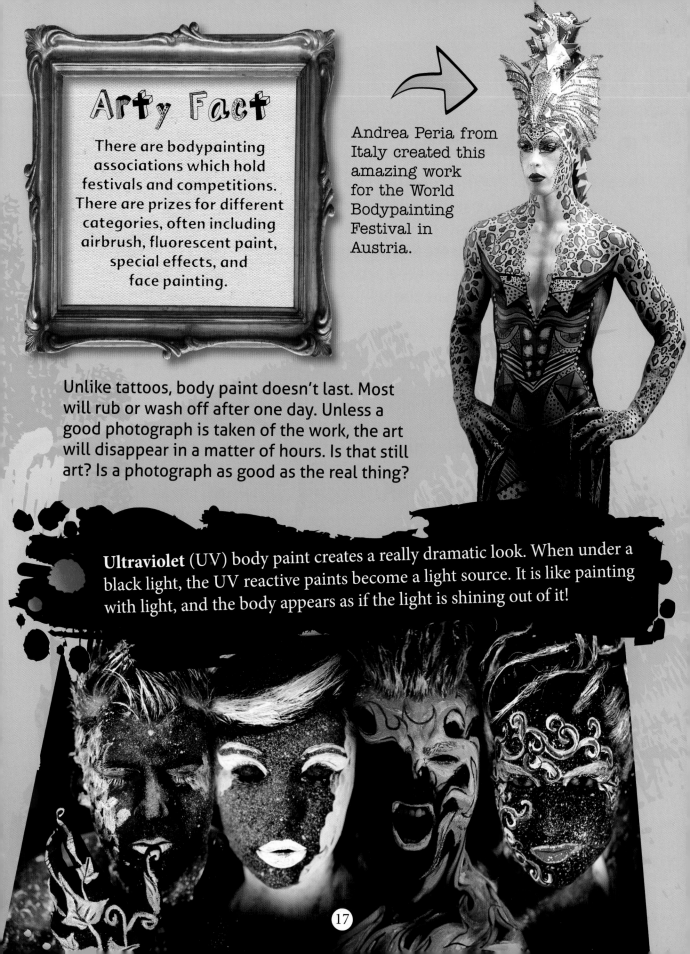

Arty Fact

There are bodypainting associations which hold festivals and competitions. There are prizes for different categories, often including airbrush, fluorescent paint, special effects, and face painting.

Andrea Peria from Italy created this amazing work for the World Bodypainting Festival in Austria.

Unlike tattoos, body paint doesn't last. Most will rub or wash off after one day. Unless a good photograph is taken of the work, the art will disappear in a matter of hours. Is that still art? Is a photograph as good as the real thing?

Ultraviolet (UV) body paint creates a really dramatic look. When under a black light, the UV reactive paints become a light source. It is like painting with light, and the body appears as if the light is shining out of it!

Masks

Many people create colorful masks to decorate their body. They can be worn for disguise, fun, or as part of a performance. Masks have been used in **ritual** ceremonies since ancient times. Masks are used in the arts, such as in the theater, but are they art themselves?

This stone mask is 9000 years old!

Some masks are made using great artistic skill. The artists usually train as an apprentice to learn their craft. Masks can be made from just about any material. They can be carved from wood or stone, or made from cloth, cardboard, or even paper.

WHAT DO YOU THINK?

Masks change your body's appearance, but they do not permanently alter your body. You can take them off at any time. Are masks really body art? If a mask is body art, can your clothes be body art, too?

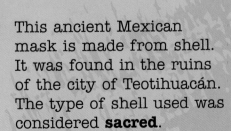

This ancient Mexican mask is made from shell. It was found in the ruins of the city of Teotihuacán. The type of shell used was considered **sacred**.

A carnival held in Venice, Italy is famous for its highly decorated masks. The maskmakers are important people in the city. Venetian masks usually have **ornate** designs with bright colors such as gold or silver. They are sometimes decorated with feathers or jewels.

Arty Fact

One reason for wearing a mask is to pretend to be someone or something else. A mask allows the wearer to adopt a new personality. Try making a scary mask and wear it for a while. Do you feel more powerful?

Masks can make people look fierce. Mexican lucha libre wrestlers wear masks. Each wrestler wears a unique design. The mask makes the wrestler look more ferocious and helps hide any fear or pain he may feel.

A lucha libre wrestler wearing his mask.

Art Using Your Body!

You can use your body to create art in a variety of inventive ways! Some people create art using their body parts, such as by finger painting or making hand prints. Other types of art can be a little more extreme. Millie Brown creates art by vomiting paint!

Millie Brown doesn't eat anything for two days before she starts "painting." She then drinks colored milk and vomits each color onto the canvas to create her artwork. She does this in front of audiences, sometimes accompanied by music. Her paintings sell for large sums of money! Brown was once filmed performing her art for a Lady Gaga music video.

WHAT DO YOU THINK?

Is vomiting paint art? Brown has limited control over where the paint will go, and she needs very little artistic skill. But she does choose the colors. She also creatively invented a whole new way of putting paint on paper!

Brown's painting *Nexus Vomitus* sold for $2,400!

Brown explained why she created her vomit paintings. "I wanted to use my body to create art, I wanted it to truly come from within, to create something beautiful that was raw and uncontrollable."

Tony Orrico is a human **Spirograph™**! His performance drawings can take up to seven hours to complete. He holds sticks of charcoal in his hands and moves his body, making symmetrical shapes, to create his patterns.

Tony Orrico used to be a dancer, and uses large body movements to create his work.

Arty Fact

When Japanese artist Hananuma Masakichi thought he was dying, he pulled out his own hair, nails, and teeth to create a sculpture of his own body! He wanted to leave a perfect replica of himself for his girlfriend. He didn't actually die for ten years, by which time his girlfriend had left!

Some artists paint using body parts. Usually people use their fingers, hands, or feet. Some artists like to roll around in the paint, too!

Can Makeup Be Art?

Makeup artists apply makeup for theater, television, film, fashion, and magazines. Day-to-day makeup probably couldn't be called art. Makeup artists can take that a step further, however, and create amazing designs that really could be seen as art.

Which one of these makeup artists is creating art? Or are they both?

Arty Fact

Award ceremonies such as the Oscars and the Emmys give out awards for top film and television makeup artists.

WHAT DO YOU THINK?

People wear makeup because they feel it makes them look better. If what you are doing is making something look good, then that must be art, right?

Everyday makeup usually simply enhances the features that a person already has. But makeup can be used to create really elaborate designs too. Catwalk models often are given crazy, attention-grabbing looks. The makeup can reflect the image the fashion house wants to give, and help get the designer noticed.

A little like a sculptor, a makeup artist needs to design a look that suits the face from many different angles.

Face paint art can be very skillful. Try creating some art on your face, and see what you can turn yourself into. If you're **allergic** to face paint, try printing out a large photo of your face and drawing on that instead!

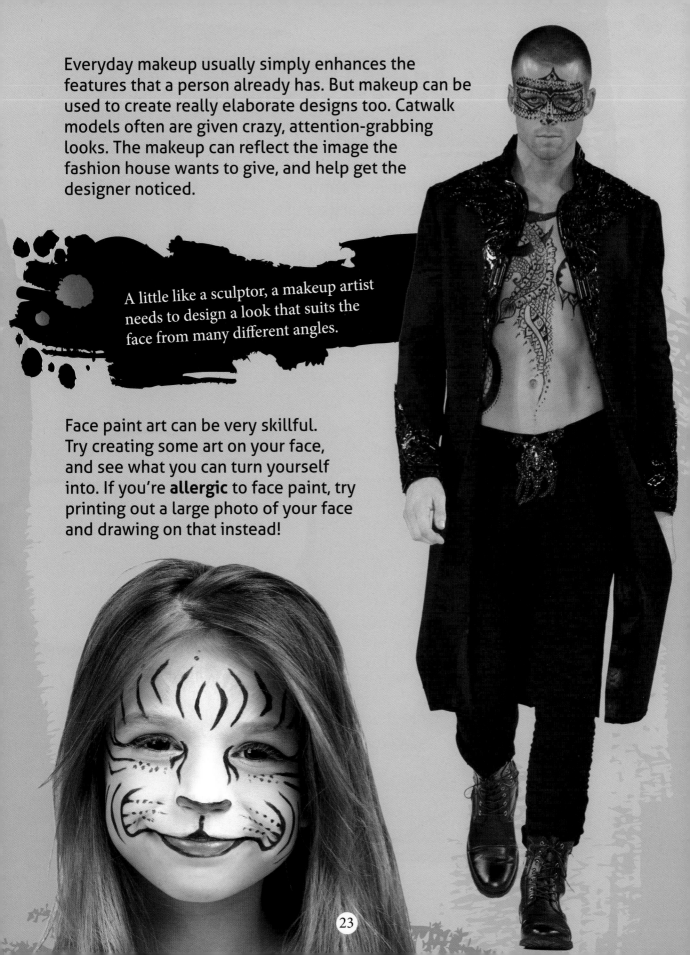

Special Effects

Not all makeup is used to make people beautiful! Movie special effects artists use **cosmetics** and **prosthetics** to create anything from an alien to a zombie! Prosthetics are pieces of flexible material placed on actors' faces to transform their appearance. Made from latex or silicone, they look very realistic!

A hobbit ear prosthetic from the movie *Lord of the Rings*.

Special effects artists create many effects using a special wax that looks like skin. To make a wound like the one below, special effects artists take a piece of the fake skin and slice it to create the cut. Then they attach the cut to the actor's arm using spirit gum. They blend the edges and paint it with a matching skin tone. Fake blood finishes the look!

WHAT DO YOU THINK?

Special effects makeup artists have to be creative. Sometimes they need to think up and create incredible creatures. They need great artistic skill to do what they do. But is what they do actually art? Or is it just a job?

A very realistic special effects wound on an actor's arm. Artists need to study real cuts to make their work look as real as possible.

Special effect Lion Man makeup by Rayce Bird, winner of the 2012 reality TV series *Face Off*. In the show, makeup artists competed against each other.

Some movie makeovers take hours to create every day. The 1980 movie *The Elephant Man* won an Academy Award for best makeup. Actor John Hurt could eat nothing from midmorning until around midnight. It took hours to put the makeup on, and then another hour and a half to take the makeup off!

Try making a special effects bruise yourself. Look at photos of actual bruises, first. Put some white makeup on the bruise area. Using a makeup brush or sponge, put on some red makeup. Start light and get darker in patches. Pat or press it onto the skin. You want it to look a little patchy. Then add purple, blue, and green makeup. Finally blend the colors with a light layer of yellow.

Body Modification

Art and beauty have always been linked. Through history people have tried modifying their bodies to look more beautiful. The Kayan people of Thailand wear neck rings to make their necks longer. The rings don't really stretch the neck, they push down on the shoulders, making the neck seem longer.

A young Kayan girl wearing neck rings.

Different people have very different ideas about what is art. The same is true about beauty. Mursi women from Ethiopia wear large pottery or wooden discs in their lower lips. The girls' lips are pierced at the age of 15 or 16. The hole is stretched by gradually inserting bigger plates, very similar to the modern trend of earlobe stretching using flesh tunnels.

a modern flesh tunnel

A Mursi woman wearing her decorated disc.

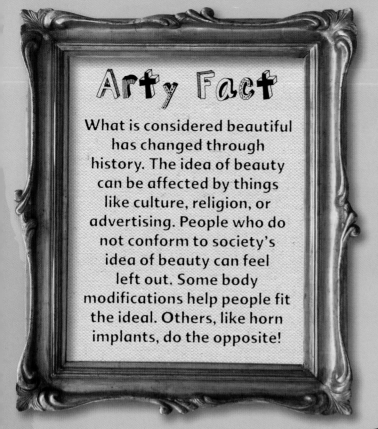

Arty Fact

What is considered beautiful has changed through history. The idea of beauty can be affected by things like culture, religion, or advertising. People who do not conform to society's idea of beauty can feel left out. Some body modifications help people fit the ideal. Others, like horn implants, do the opposite!

Some people love to experiment with body art. New technologies such as glow-in-the-dark tattoos and implants have involved modern science in the art. Implants such as the horns in the picture below are created by inserting small pieces of teflon, coral, or silicone under the skin. As the skin stretches, they may add more material to make the horns larger!

Implants can certainly create an unusual effect!

WHAT DO YOU THINK?

Body art can be fun. It's exciting being creative with your looks. But you can't control how people respond to how you look. Do you think some body art might be a bad idea? Could it prevent you from getting a job, for instance?

If you think about it, even going to the gym is a form of body modification. Bodybuilders put their body under stress so that they can sculpt it into a shape that they think looks better!

Is Body Art Art?

Have you made up your mind? Is body art art? To help you, have a look at some of these arguments "for" and "against."

Body Art IS Art

- It's called body art, so it must be art
- It's a way for people to express themselves
- It can help to improve people's appearance
- The artists think what they are doing is art
- Museums and galleries sometimes display body art installations, or photographs of body art
- Body art is used in other forms of art, such as film and theater
- Body art is probably the oldest type of art

Body Art ISN'T Art

- Body art can look ugly
- Many people don't like to look at body art
- Body art is more about culture and tradition than art
- Some body art is done to shock, not to look good
- Theater or fashion makeup artists often just copy a look rather than create something new
- If making holes in people is art, why isn't a surgeon an artist too?
- Vomiting paint doesn't need much skill, so how can it be art?

Arty Fact

Sometimes body art can keep people from doing what they want to do. Most people don't associate body art with professional job positions. It's not a good idea to display body art at a job interview.

Because body art is seen as shocking by some people, it has an exciting **edgy** feel to it. Methods of making body art keep developing which keeps the art new and creative. It can be temporary or permanent, happy and colorful, or dark and disturbing. Body art can help turn an ordinary body into something unique and personal.

In many ways, body art is one of the best forms of art. You can take your art with you every day. Body art can be seen by many more people than the same art on the wall of your house would be seen by.

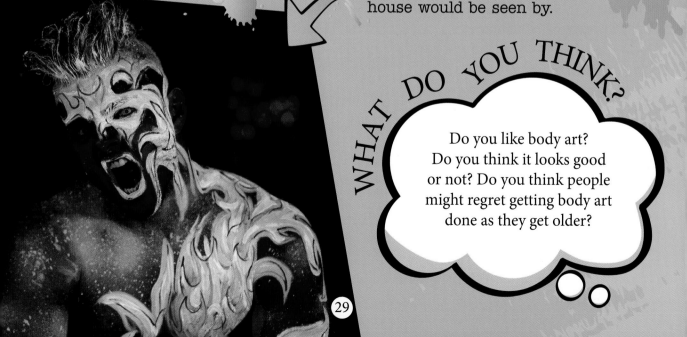

WHAT DO YOU THINK?

Do you like body art? Do you think it looks good or not? Do you think people might regret getting body art done as they get older?

Glossary

allergic
Have an allergy to something.

apprentice
A person who is learning a trade or art by experience under a skilled worker.

camouflage
Hiding or disguising something by covering it up or changing the way it looks.

cosmetics
Makeup.

culture
A group of people who share the same beliefs and ways of life.

edgy
At the forefront of a trend; experimental or avant-garde.

Hindu
A follower of Hinduism.

nonconformist
A person who, in their behavior or views, does not conform to normal ideas or practices in their community.

ornate
Having a lot of decoration.

prosthetics
Pieces of flexible material applied to actors' faces to transform their appearance.

rite of passage
A ceremony or event marking an important stage in someone's life, especially birth, the transition from childhood to adulthood, marriage, and death.

ritual
A formal ceremony.

sacred
Holy, or deserving respect or honor.

spiritual
Of or relating to sacred or religious matters.

Spirograph™
A toy used to draw intricate curved patterns using interlocking plastic cogs and toothed rings of different sizes.

status
Position or rank in relation to others.

typography
The style and appearance of printed matter.

ultraviolet
The ultraviolet part of the color spectrum.

unique
Being the only one of its kind.

For More Information

Books

Claybourne, Anna. *Piercing*. Portsmouth, NH: Heinemann Library, 2005.

Claybourne, Anna. *Body Painting*. Portsmouth, NH: Heinemann Library, 2005.

Noble, Marty. *Mehndi Designs Coloring Book: Traditional Henna Body Art*. Mineola, NY: Dover Children's, 2013.

Websites

Art Symphony
http://artsymphony.blogspot.co.uk/2013/03/body-art-using-painted-hands.html
Great images of Guido Daniele's body paint hands.

Nailpolis
http://www.nailpolis.com
A showcase of great inspirational nail art from around the world.

Publisher's note to educators and parents:
Our editors have carefully reviewed these websites to ensure that they are suitable for students. Many websites change frequently, however, and we cannot guarantee that a site's future contents will continue to meet our high standards of quality and educational value. Be advised that students should be closely supervised whenever they access the Internet.

Index

B
Bird, Rayce 25

body modification 26, 27
body paint 16, 17
body piercings 12, 13
Brown, Millie 20, 21

D
Davidson, Elaine 13

F
face paint 16, 23
folk art 9

H
henna tattoos 8, 9

I
implants 27

J
James, Greg 10

K
Karo tribe 4
Kayan people 26
Khond women 12

M
makeup 4, 6, 22, 23
Masakichi, Hananuma 21
masks 4, 6, 18, 19
Mayans 6
Mursi women 26

N
nail art 5, 14

O
Orrico, Tony 21

P
Peria, Andrew 17
prosthetics 24

S
special effects 17, 24, 25

T
tattoos 4, 5, 6, 7, 10, 11, 15, 17
teeth art 14, 15